ELVIS LEGENDS ALPHABET

Words by Robin Feiner

A is for **Al**ways On My Mind
The King of Rock 'n' Roll
recorded this legendary tune
shortly after separating from
Priscilla, his wife, in 1970.
His tender and loving heart
bursts open with every
crooning lyric: 'Maybe
I didn't love you, quite as
often as I could have. Maybe
I didn't treat you, quite as
good as I should have.'

B is for **B**lue Suede Shoes. Presley had a storied history of collaborating with Black artists and covering their hit songs. 'Blue Suede Shoes'—made a hit by Carl Perkins in 1955 and then a megahit by Presley in '56—was all about busting a move and keeping those dancing shoes clean the whole night through.

C is for Don't Be **C**ruel.
The King was playful, bashful, and full of wild, tender love. Nowhere do those traits shine more than on this legendary tune written by his good friend Otis Blackwell. Released alongside 'Hound Dog' in '56, it remains the only single to have both sides go number one on the Billboard charts.

D is for Hound **D**og.
'You ain't nothin' but a hound dog, cryin' all the time.' Are there better-known lyrics in the history of music? This hit was so everlasting it was inducted into the Grammy Hall of Fame in 1988, years after Elvis' passing. Speaking of Grammys, the King won three of them.

E is for **E**arly Morning Rain. It's no surprise that Elvis was adored by all—including the artists whose songs he covered. Gordon Lightfoot, the original singer of this legendary slow song, said Elvis' rendition was his favorite cover of any of his songs. 'In the early morning rain with a dollar in my hand ...'

F is for Can't Help **F**alling In Love. Anyone itching for love can just play their crush this 1961 smash hit and watch as their eyes turn to hearts. It's regarded as one of the most romantic songs ever penned. 'Like a river flows, surely to the sea. Darling, so it goes, some things are meant to be.'

G is for In the **G**hetto. Recorded in '69, this tragic tale of a poor child 'in the ghetto' became Elvis' first Top 10 hit in four years, announcing his glorious return to stardom. A true legend, he was always thinking of those less fortunate. No wonder he was awarded the Presidential Medal of Freedom.

H is for Heartbreak Hotel. While Elvis was already cool in '56, 'Heartbreak Hotel' was his first number-one hit on the Billboard 100 charts, making him more of a global sensation. If fans across the pond hadn't already been exposed to his gyrating hips and risqué nature, they certainly were after this.

I is for Devil In Disguise. 'You look like an angel ... walk like an angel ... talk like an angel ... but I got wise ... you're the devil in disguise.' This devilish tune reached number one on the UK charts and number three on the US charts, and it was a legendary fan favorite when Elvis performed in Vegas, where he played over 600 shows.

J is for Jailhouse Rock. Easily regarded as one of the King's greatest songs, this megahit was released in 1957 alongside his film of the same name. In the film, Elvis performs one of his most elaborate dance numbers, twisting, tippy-toeing, and sliding down a fire pole— all while belting, 'Everybody, let's rock.'

K is for **K**entucky Rain.
Born in Mississippi and raised
partially in Tennessee, Elvis
had a deep love for the
Southern states. Written by
the great Eddie Rabbitt, this
legendary track shows the
King at his most vulnerable,
with lyrics that find him
searching the streets of
Kentucky for a lost lover.

L is for Love Me Tender.
Throw on this tearjerker from
1956 and let the tears flow.
It was the theme song for the
first of Elvis' 31 movies, and it
was what the King performed
during his first appearance
on The Ed Sullivan Show. Like
many of his hits, it reached
number one on Billboard's
Hot 100.

Mm

M is for **M**ystery Train.
Of the legendary lesser-
known tracks Elvis recorded,
'Mystery Train' was his best.
Rolling Stone ranked his
version number 77 on their
500 Greatest Songs of All Time
list. The tune was fast, upbeat,
and always in rhythm—just like
the King. 'Train, train, comin'
'round, 'round the bend.'

N is for It's Now or Never. In a 1961 press conference, Elvis said that this song was his favorite of all the ones he'd recorded. His legendary deep voice on the tune would make crowds of screaming, adoring fans clutch their hearts. 'Kiss me, my darling, be mine tonight. Tomorrow will be too late.'

Oo

O is for **O**ne Night.
This song reached number one on the UK charts way back in 1959. Decades later, in 2005, the track again reached the top spot after being rereleased to honor Presley's 70th birthday. Far surpassing his 'one night with you,' the King has retained status as a musical icon.

P is for Elvis **P**resley. Graceland's King of Rock 'n' Roll was all gyrating hips, love songs, and pure charisma. He went from a small-time Mississippi native to the best-selling solo artist of all time, with the most gold and platinum hit albums to boot. He's the greatest one-man act ever to live, and a true legend.

Q is for Kiss Me **Q**uick.
This smaller Elvis hit was like
many others: pure, romantic,
and easy to dance to. It saw
the King singing to a lover he
wanted to be with for eternity:
'Tell me that tonight will last
forever, say that you will
leave me never. Kiss me
quick because I love you so.'

R is for **R**eturn to Sender. In concert, the King sang this track with his legendary hips swaying back and forth and his fingers snapping to the beat. As usual, he slicked back his shining black hair and donned the coolest whites ever sewn. 'Return to sender, address unknown. No such person, no such zone.'

S is for **S**uspicious Minds.
By the end of the '60s,
Beatlemania had swept the
world and Elvis was nearing
the latter stages of his career.
But in 1969, he reclaimed the
spotlight with the legendary
'Suspicious Minds.' It was his
first number-one US hit since
1962, and overnight the
world had fallen in love
with him again.

T is for An American **T**rilogy. This legendary epic unites three unsung Elvis hits: 'Dixie,' 'Battle Hymn of the Republic,' and 'All My Trials.' The King performed the three songs together to unite America during a time of political tension. Priscilla Presley called this song and 'If I Can Dream' her favorite Elvis tunes.

U is for All Shook **Up.**
It's impossible to hear this track without wanting to thrust your hips and rip out your air guitar—just like our 'all shook up' King. When it was released, Elvis was having the hottest streak an artist has ever known, with nine different songs spending 50 combined weeks atop Billboard's singles list!

V is for **V**iva Las Vegas. Vegas is known for being the wildest city in the entire United States. No wonder the King loved it there—he was all about taking risks and smashing rock 'n' roll barriers. He played shows daily in Sin City during the latter stages of his career. 'Bright light city gonna set my soul, gonna set my soul on fire.'

W is for The **W**onder of You. Elvis concerts were the stuff of legend, and this track was one the King belted out triumphantly in almost every concert he performed at. 'And you're always there to lend a hand, in everything I do.' The women who packed his concerts, all liked to dream the King was talking to them.

X is for A Little Less Conversation, Junkie **XL** Remix. Elvis passed away in 1977. Years later, his legendary music was still being played and remixed to glorious reception. In 2002, Junkie XL remixed 'A Little Less Conversation.' With an entirely new audience introduced to The King, the song soared to number 1 in 24 countries across the globe.

Y is for Are **Y**ou Lonesome Tonight? In 1960, Presley was known as a rock star. He wanted to show audiences he was capable of more. So, he slowed his rhythm and recorded this gutpunch of a love song. 'Does your memory stray to a bright summer day when I kissed you and called you sweetheart?'

Z is for Signs of the Zodiac. Elvis was a notorious Capricorn. The goat is hard-working, ambitious, and destined for greatness, just like the King. Whether he was ripping the guitar, calmly playing piano, or belting out a tune, he always did it with pride. As the lyrics go: 'Tony is a Capricorn, a leader of men.'

The ever-expanding legendary library

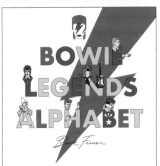

EXPLORE THESE LEGENDARY ALPHABETS & MORE AT WWW.ALPHABETLEGENDS.COM

ELVIS LEGENDS ALPHABET
www.alphabetlegends.com

Published by Alphabet Legends Pty Ltd in 2022
Created by Beck Feiner
Copyright © Alphabet Legends Pty Ltd 2022

Printed and bound in China.

9780645487060

ALPHABET LEGENDS